What Do You Think?

A Study of
Philippians 4

by Betty S. Bender

ISBN: 0-89098-317-8

Scripture quotations are from the New International Version,
1973, 1978, 1984 by International Bible Society

DEDICATION

To the memory of Duane whose life portrayed love and laughter which he shared with me for forty nine and half years as I saw him teach others how to love as God loves. Although he has finished his course and moved on to higher realms, his teaching lives on in the hearts of many he taught.

My Gratitude

To the ladies' class in Anderson, SC who encouraged me when I first led them in a study of the material,

To Porter and Judy King who read the manuscript and made suggestions,

To Vickie Cofer who contributed her time and talent to get it ready for print,

To her husband, Steve, who lended his words of encouragement and financial support,

And to God, the Father, who has provided me with many opportunities to learn of Him,

I will be eternally thankful.

ORGANIZATION

❋

These lessons from Philippians 4 are designed for a small group study. The purpose is for each participant to take part in the class session and then intently put into practice the concept discussed in class. The encouragement of others in the group who have the same intent assists each one in her effort to remember and practice that concept daily during the following week.

To work most effectively, groups should be limited to ten people. If more than ten wish to participate, a second leader should be selected and the group divided. **These small group studies are suitable for those who desire group study in addition to a regular Bible class.** It is important to keep the groups small enough to be accommodated in a home setting which is conducive to more intimate interaction. This will also encourage participants to be open and honest and share their lives as they put this learning experience into practice. The success of these studies hinges on the group getting close enough through prayer and concern for each other that everyone feels comfortable to open up and share their experiences

This study can be adapted to be used in a regular Bible class. The entire group could meet together for prayer and singing, then divide into small groups in various classrooms with various members serving as small group leaders. In one congregation where I used this study, we started with only one group of four women. When we completed the first study, each of the participants voluntarily became leaders with a newly formed group. Within a year, over half of the ladies in the congregation were involved in on-going groups.

In a neighborhood setting, this study can be used to involve those who are not Christians. Any individual who desires to start a group study can act as a leader and recruit a few others to participate.

GETTING STARTED

❋

At the first session, the leader will ask each participant to sign the commitment below in her study guide. This will encourage each one to make a serious effort to be consistent in attendance which will be conducive to all growing closer to God during the thirteen week study.

I agree to be present for all thirteen sessions of this study, <u>What Do You Think?</u> unless I am ill or otherwise unable. I agree to be accountable to the other members of the group to be an active participant in practicing the teaching of each week's lesson and to share my experiences at the next class session.

Signed_____

It is important to begin on time and try to close as near on time as possible. This will encourage those who have other commitments to take part. If refreshments are served, wait until after the closing prayer and those who need to leave may do so without missing any part of the study. However, when possible, it is a good idea to encourage participants to visit afterwards to get to know each other better. This will produce further opportunity for them to share their blessings and their struggles with one another.

It is suggested that each participant use the space provided for notes which will include:
1. Prayer concerns of the group and notes about answered prayers.
2. Notes taken during the lesson each week.
3. Notes made about the successes and/or struggles of carrying out the assignment for the week.

FORMAT FOR STUDY SESSIONS

❀

The group leader will prepare for the study. Sitting around a table is preferable. If this is not feasible, then chairs should be arranged close together in a circle.

Although this is a discussion type study, it will be the responsibility of the leader to give the short lesson each week, as well as keep the group focused on the purpose of the study. Because there will be much discussion, this will give rise to talkative participants taking up too much time and drifting off the subject. The leader should be prepared to step in at any point and kindly suggest getting back to the lesson of the day. She should also watch for those who are quiet and not entering into the discussion. She might call a name and ask that person a specific question in order to encourage each one to participate. In some cases, the leader will find it appropriate to go around the circle, asking each one to answer a question from her experiences of the week.

Suggested format is as follows:
1. Discussing prayer requests and prayers answered.
2. Time of prayer.
3. Each member reports on week's activities
4. Group leader introduces lesson.
5. Discussion of lesson and answering questions.
6. Group leader makes assignment for following week.

SCHEDULE

❀

Session 1   Introduction–in the first session the group leader will introduce the concept of this study of Philippians 4

Session 2   Stand Firm in the Lord

Session 3   Whatever is true

Session 4   Whatever is noble

Session 5   Whatever is right

Session 6   Whatever is pure

Session 7   Whatever is lovely

Session 8   Whatever is admirable

Session 9   Whatever is excellent or praiseworthy

For the remaining four weeks in the quarter, the lessons will come from the verses following Philippians 4:8:

Session 10 Putting our thoughts into practice,

Session 11 Being content in the place we find ourselves,

Session 12 Doing all things through Christ

Session 13 God's promise to meet all our needs

Following the last session: A good ending for this course is sharing a buffet together, giving each participant opportunity to summarize what she has gained from participation in the course and how it has affected her life.

Discuss the course, its lasting meaning, and things we can anticipate as we continue to practice what we have learned.

TRANSLATIONS OF DIFFERENT VERSIONS

❀

KJV	**TRUE**	Honest	Just	Pure
AS	**TRUE**	Honorable	Just	Pure
NAS	**TRUE**	Honorable	Just	Pure
NIV	**TRUE**	Noble	Right	Pure
RSV	**TRUE**	Honorable	Just	Pure
NEB	**TRUE**	Noble	Just	Pure
TEV	**TRUE**	Noble	Right	Pure
JERU	**TRUE**	Noble	Right	Pure
PHIL	**TRUE**	Honorable	Just	Pure
LB	**TRUE**	Good	Right	Pure

Words from Philippians 4:8

Lovely	Good Report	Virtue	Praise
Lovely	Good Report	Virtue	Praise
Lovely	Good Repute	Excellence	Praise
Lovely	Admirable	Excellent	Worthy of praise
Lovely	Gracious	Excellent	Praiseworthy
Lovable	Gracious	Excellent	Admirable
Lovely	Honorable	Good	Deserve praise
We love	Honor	Thought virtuous	Worthy of Praise
Lovely	Admirable	Goodness	Value approval of God
Lovely	Good	Be glad about	Praise God for

TABLE OF CONTENTS

❀

SESSION 1

❀

INTRODUCTION

The purpose of this group study is to grow closer to God as we look at what His word tells us about what we should think. As we come together each week to consider this, we will also get to know each other better, learn to love each other more, and encourage one another to love and good works.

Our thoughts are the beginning process of all we do and how we live. When the Pharisees were questioning Jesus in Matthew 12, he told them if a tree is good then its fruit will be good for a tree is recognized by its fruit. He further told them "...how can you who are evil say anything good? For out of the overflow of the heart the mouth speaks. The good man brings good things out of the good stored up in him, and the evil man brings evil things out of the evil stored up in him (vss. 33-35).

Find three additional scriptures which support the fact that our thoughts must be pure before our lives are right with God.

a.

b.

c.

In order for our words to be wholesome and our works to be good, the thoughts of our heart must be wholesome. The beginning place for a rich spiritual life is with the things we think, the thoughts we dwell on each day. If we think positive thoughts we are going to be optimistic, pleasant and productive for the Lord.

Do you find it difficult to keep your thoughts on spiritual things?
Yes____ No____
Give a reason for your answer.

The ways of the world entice us to think of things which are not according to God's ways. List three things which keep your thoughts from always being what God would want them to be.

a.

b.

c.

As we begin this study together, we will make a commitment to be present every week and be a positive encouragement to the group. Does God consider a commitment we make to others to be binding?

Yes____ No____.

How seriously do you take a commitment that you make?

What deterrents do you foresee you may have to overcome to keep this commitment?

List ways you overcome these deterrents.

3

Prayers Answered:

_____
_____
_____
_____
_____
_____
_____
_____
_____
_____

Prayer Requests: _____

_____
_____
_____
_____
_____
_____
_____
_____
_____
_____
_____

Memory Verse:

_____

_____

_____

_____

_____

_____

_____

_____

_____

_____

SESSION 2

❃

STAND FIRM IN THE LORD

Philippians 4:1-7

1. Begin this first session with a short prayer by the leader. In the following weeks, you may begin class with prayer requests and discussion of needs of each member. Leader will explain the format for the weekly sessions together and ask each one to sign the commitment on page II. It should be emphasized that each class builds on the previous ones, and regular attendance is very important. Leader may want to remind the group from time to time of this commitment

2. Go around the circle and each participant tells of her study needs at this time—or what she hopes to gain from the study.

3. Discuss prayer needs and requests of group (list on pg. 15).

4. Time of prayer. Give each class member opportunity to pray by using a chain prayer. (Hold hands to pray, and if someone doesn't feel comfortable praying aloud, she may simply squeeze the next person's hand when it is her turn, and this will be a cue for the next person to continue.)

LEADER PRESENTS LESSON

Philippians 4:1-7

As we study Paul's final chapter in his letter to the Philippians, we can feel his heartfelt desire for them to be close to each other and to grow together in the Lord. In this study we are going to try to do just what Paul is asking the Philippians to do.

Paul tells this church that he loves them dearly and he admonishes them to "stand firm in the Lord," to be at peace and to live exemplary lives so others will be drawn to God by their example.

How can we follow this advice today?

It is important that we spend time with those who will help us to resist the devil and to do what is right.

How does thinking right help us to stand firm in the Lord as Paul advises in Philippians 4:1?

He urges two sisters who have been very effective in standing with him for the "cause of the gospel" to overcome their difficulties and continue to work with others "whose names are written in the book of life." As we consider Euodia and Syntyche, let's remember their good works. Often these two good sisters are **condemned** because they are having a disagreement, but Paul **commends** them for their labors with him and says their names are in the book of life (Phil. 4:2,3).

What hinders us from "agreeing with each other in the Lord" (vs. 2) and how can we overcome these hindrances?

Is it possible for us to always keep a right relationship with everyone?

What can we do to improve?

Paul stresses the importance of our being happy in the Lord. For emphasis, he repeats his command to "Rejoice!" (Philippians 4:4). Indeed we can be happy in the Lord, even when Satan is throwing darts from every side — if we are able to stand firm. By sharing our trials and hardships, and yes, even our joys, we build one another up.

How will learning to center our thoughts on the right things help us to rejoice (Philippians 4:4)?

Paul wants the Philippians to rejoice always, living an example to others by being gentle (Philippians 4:5). He wants us to practice gentleness to everyone, just as Jesus practiced gentleness with the woman taken in adultery (John 8:3-11).

He tells the Philippians not to be anxious about anything. When others see Christians staying calm and composed when their world is crashing in around them, they take notice. Write an example of you seeing this happen in your life or the life of someone you know.

Turning everything over to God in prayer is the way to avoid anxiety. He takes care of our problems when we can't. And when we let Him, He guards our hearts and minds to keep worry and anxiety out and gives us that "peace which transcends all understanding," which "guards our hearts and minds in Christ Jesus" (Philippians 4:6, 7).

How will thinking the right thoughts take away our anxiety and help us to have peace with God?

Paul tells us what to think in order to live as we should (Philippians 4:8). All of our actions begin with the thoughts we think. Norman Vincent Peale said: "Change your thoughts and you change your world." Jesus said: **"Out of the overflow of the heart the mouth speaks" (Matthew 12:34).** He further told them if a tree is good then its fruit will be good, for a tree is recognized by its fruit (Matthew 12:33). If we are living good lives, it starts with thinking good thoughts.

Discuss how our thoughts can help us bear good fruit.

Our thoughts precede and determine our actions. A very successful way to change our thoughts is by "thought transferal." When we think something negative about someone or some thing, immediately we need to change that thought to something positive and dwell on that long enough for it to crowd out the negative and become well ingrained in our mind. Thought transferal will be a good practice for us throughout this course as we try to think more the way Paul instructs in Philippians 4:8. Let's remind each other often of our need for thought transferal.

In order for our words to be wholesome and our works to be good, the thoughts of our heart must be wholesome. The beginning place for a rich spiritual life is with the things we think; the thoughts we dwell on every day. If we think positive thoughts, we are going to be optimistic, pleasant and productive for the Lord.

DISCUSSION

Is it difficult to keep your thoughts on spiritual things? Yes_____
No_____
Give a reason for your answer.

List the things which keep your thoughts from always being what God would want them to be.

In your own words, write what the following scriptures mean to you.

Matthew 9:4

James 1:7

James 4:5-7

Proverbs 23:7

Romans 12:3

Matthew 26:65-66

How does I Thessalonians 3:12 tell us we can help each other to have a joyful spirit?

Beginning next week, in each class session we will concentrate on "thinking" on one of the things Paul lists in Philippians 4:8. We will try to practice thinking positively on that attribute and putting it into action throughout the week. At the beginning of each class session, we will each report the results from the following week.

Assignment for this week: Read Philippians every day. Although our course is centered on Philippians 4, a better understanding of the entire book will help us to understand Paul's message in this verse. Make notes about what you hope to gain from this study and any questions you'd like for the group to discuss.

Memory verse for this week: I Corinthians 11:1

Leader closes with prayer.

Prayers Answered:

_____
_____
_____
_____
_____
_____
_____
_____
_____
_____

Prayer Requests: _____

_____
_____
_____
_____
_____
_____
_____
_____
_____
_____
_____
_____

Memory Verse:

_____

_____

_____

_____

_____

_____

_____

_____

_____

_____

SESSION 3
❋
THINK ON THINGS TRUE
PHILIPPIANS 4:8

1. Leader may assign scriptures to be read aloud in class when she calls for them.

2. Allow time for writing memory verse in notebook.

3. Each participant gives report on prayers answered and prayer requests of group (List on page 27).

4. Time of prayer. Give each one who desires opportunity to pray aloud.

5. Go around circle and each participant tell what she gained from reading the book of Philippians every day.

LEADER PRESENTS LESSON
Read Philippians 4:8

As we begin this journey together through Philippians 4:8, we will want to make every effort to practice the concept of the week's word every time we have opportunity. Our goal is to become so aware of this concept that we will continue to practice it more fully than we ever have after the week of intense effort is over.

Jesus prayed for his disciples in John: "Sanctify them by the truth; your word is truth" (John 17:17).

17

How would you define truth?

In John 18:37, Jesus told Pilate: "For this reason I came into the world, to testify to the truth. Everyone on the side of truth listens to me." Then Pilate asked: "What is truth?"

The Greek word for truth as used in Philippians 4:8 is defined as follows: "Real, actual, appearance is not mere show, but is the reality it appears to be. Utterance agrees with the reality and does not conceal that reality."

How does God compare a half-truth with a lie?

What we want to practice this week is telling the truth, the whole truth and nothing but the truth.
Discuss each of the following:
evading the truth

or trying to justify slanting the truth to fit your purposes or telling the portion of truth which will make you look better

or stretching the truth to make your story more phenomenal.

All of us can probably think of times we have been guilty of some of these things.

According to I John 5:20, how can we discern what is true?

During this week we want to be aware of what we say and be very careful to keep within the realm of what is real and actual.

Read John 7:16-18
To whom should we be true?

Jesus teaches us in John 7:16-18 that we are to be true to God first. He set the example for us. He said He worked for the honor of the one who sent him and he is truth (vs. 18). We are working for the same God that Jesus did, and we also need to work for His honor.

19

In our everyday life, how careful are we to always tell the whole truth?

Why do we often find this hard to do?

In John 18:28-29, the Jews who brought Jesus before Pilate were trying hard to evade the truth. When Pilate asked what charges they brought against Jesus, they evaded his question by saying Pilate surely knew he was a criminal or they would not bring him to Pilate (vs. 30). Pilate tried to evade his responsibility to search out the truth by shifting the burden back on them when he told them to judge Jesus by their own law (vs. 31).

What kind of character do you see Pilate displaying in trying to shift the blame?

The Jews had put Pilate in a dilemma. When he questioned Jesus (vss. 33-37), He told him that He had come into the world to testify to the truth. Then Pilate asked that profound question, "What is truth?"

I believe that Pilate was confused at this time about what the actual truth was. Or perhaps he was trying to stall for time—or put Jesus in a dilemma. The Jews had Pilate exactly where they wanted him. They had confused the issue to keep the truth from being evident.

Why do you think Pilate asked this question?

Sometimes we can also become confused. Have you ever known people who lie so often that it seems doubtful if they know when they are lying? I had a student who often lied when it would have been better for her to tell the truth. I believe she had lied so much without being corrected for it that she was confused about what the truth really was. If we always strive to tell the truth, we won't find ourselves in this dilemma. This is a practical reason why we should always practice the truth.

What other reasons can you think of?

How would you answer if someone asked you, "What is truth?"

Read Psalms 33:4; Psalm 119:160
According to these verses why is truth so important?

Our guide for discerning truth is the Scriptures. I John tells us that Christ has given us understanding that we may know Him who is true.

Read Ephesians 4:15, 29
Write its meaning in your words.

Although we are to always tell the truth, we want to be kind about it. We will "grow up in Christ" if we follow His example to speak kindly even if we must speak words that are hard for another to accept.

Is there ever a time we should not tell the "whole truth? Explain your answer.

Read Acts 20:32
Explain in your words.

There is some truth that can be hurtful if told at the wrong time and/or in the wrong setting. Mature Christians speak the truth in love and only when it builds others up.
Give an example of truth that is hurtful if told at the wrong time or place.

Read Matthew 27:14; John:3-6; Matthew 21:23-27
What do these scriptures teach us?

Sometimes it is best if we remain quiet or refuse to answer questions. Jesus at times refused to answer questions when His enemies were trying to trap Him.

Read Matthew 21:23-27; Mark 11:28-33; John 18:34
Capsulate the meaning of these verses.

Jesus often answered a question with a question. This can be a good strategy when you are asked to give information which might be hurtful to yourself or another.

As we grow in knowledge, we are better equipped to answer in truth and still be kind and appropriate with our answers.

What can we learn from how Jesus handled hard questions?

Let's embark on a week of truth. Be sure to note the effect as you practice truth with others and how it affects you also. Next week we will discuss the changes it has made in our lives. Perhaps you are already aware of being more truthful, and all you will need to do is just make notes below, but be sure to have something to report.

DISCUSSION

When you have trouble in being absolutely truthful and still not offending people when they ask for information that you feel you should not reveal, how do you handle it?

How does your response affect how you feel?

How can we prepare ourselves to be truthful and still not give out information that will be hurtful to someone?

How can we be honest and still not hurt people's feelings with truth?

How do you feel inwardly when you know you have lied to someone?

What do you do about those feelings?

How do you handle it when someone lies to you?

How do you respond to them?

Assignment: This week's assignment is to think on "whatever is true" and to make ourselves aware of being truthful, fully truthful in everything we say and do. It might surprise us just how often this will be a real challenge. It will help to keep account of our experiences in this, if we write down every day how we have met the challenge that day. At the first of our next class, we will each report on how being fully truthful has made a difference the past week.

Memory verse: Isaiah 32:8

Leader calls on someone to lead closing prayer.

Prayers Answered:

_____
_____
_____
_____
_____
_____
_____
_____

Prayer Requests: _____

_____
_____
_____
_____
_____
_____
_____
_____
_____
_____
_____
_____

Memory Verse:

_____

_____

_____

_____

_____

_____

_____

_____

_____

SESSION 4

❀

THINK ON THINGS NOBLE
PHILIPPIANS 4:8

1. Leader may assign scriptures to be read aloud in class when she calls for them.

2. Allow time for memory verse to be written in notebooks.

3. Each participant gives report on prayers answered and prayer requests. (List on page 39).

4. Time of prayer. Leader may call on one person to give thanks and a second to make the requests of the group.

5. Give each participant opportunity to relate experiences the past week as she practiced truthfulness.

LEADER PRESENTS LESSON

Our word this week is "noble" so we will strive to be noble in our thoughts and our deeds. "True" which we considered last week was translated "true" in every version, but our word today, "noble," is harder to translate and different versions translate it as noble, honest, honorable.

The Greek word for noble as used in Philippians 4:8 is defined as follows: **"Revered, august, venerable, grave, dignified."**

Some of these words are not commonly used today, so let's look at Webster's definition of them:

- August- Supreme dignity or grandeur, majestic, sacred.
- Venerable- Commanding respect because of age, high office or noble character.
- Grave- Solemn.
- Dignified- Marked by dignity of aspect or manner, noble, stately.

"Noble" relates to how we think about God and our fellowman, how we relate to others and how our heart feels about being upright. Let's first consider how we are noble toward God.

How do we conduct ourselves nobly toward God and toward others?

Read Hebrews 13:15
Comment the meaning of these words to you.

We relate to God nobly when we offer Him praise with our words. When we pray, we should always begin by praising and glorifying Him for who He is and all He has done for us. When we talk to others about God, we should be careful to use respectful words. Remember He is to be revered, so we speak of Him in a loftier manner than when we are speaking of men.

Recently one of my single friends called to tell me about this wonderful single preacher she had met, and when she spoke his name, I immediately knew he was someone very special to her. She called me a few weeks later about how much he meant to her and how their friendship was growing into what she hoped would be a lasting relationship.

Do you know people who so adore their mate or their child that when they speak his name, they have a different tone in their voice? This is how we should speak about God, using words of dignity and honor. As we develop a close, personal relationship with Him, we must maintain utmost respect. As we speak reverently about God, we find ourselves having more esteem for Him.

How do you address God in your prayers?

How can we help others who do not show proper respect for God without appearing "holier than thou?"

In our casual lifestyle today, we often hear God's name used disrespectfully. It has become so commonplace that many people use His name in vain without even being aware of it. As those who love and serve Him, we must realize that taking His name in vain is sinful (Exodus 20:7).

What common words are often used that seem to you as disrespectful to God?

Often jokes are told that speak of God in a flippant, careless manner. Let's guard against this as we mature in the Lord. Does this mean that we are to be somber? Gloomy? Dismal? No, God has a sense of humor, and He has given us one, but He wants us to use it to build others up and not tear them down.

How should we react when others tell "off-color" jokes?

It is especially important for Christians to guard against belittling others who may have deficiencies in their lives which they cannot help. All men were created by God, and He loves and respects each one. We should treat all men with dignity, no matter what they do.

Relate how you have seen those with handicaps or deformities mistreated.

How did that make you feel?

32

How did you react?

Read Acts 17:11
Why do you think this verse is included in God's book?

Part of developing a noble character is studying the word of God and putting it into practice. Beginning each day with God's word gets us off to a good start. We can't just accept what others say about the word. We must search for the meaning ourselves. I've often admired women who have the reputation of knowing the scripture. Many times we think it's more important for men to know God's word because they are the "public proclaimers." But we need to know in order to guide others to God, especially the younger women (Titus 2:1-5). I believe my generation has not taught the younger women as well as we should. I pray that future generations will do a better job.

Discuss how older women can teach younger women in a manner that the younger women will feel is helpful rather than critical?

Read Luke 8:15

Write in your own words.

A noble life not only means that we speak reverently of God, but that our words and actions toward our fellowman are right also. The Christian life is about having a heart that prompts us to act nobly. We must hear the word, then put it to work in our lives to bear fruit. We not only do what is expected of us, but we go above and beyond the call of duty.

In Proverbs 31 we read of the "wife of noble character." She is described as "worth far more than rubies." She brings honor to her husband (vss. 11, 12). She is industrious as she gathers food and clothing for her family (vss. 13:19, 21, 22) . She is benevolent and concerned with the poor and needy (vs.20). She lives a life that brings respect to her husband (vs. 23), she is strong and dignified, yet she has a sense of humor (vs. 25), she is wise (vs. 26), she is busy keeping her household running smoothly (vs. 27), her husband and children revere her because of her noble life (vs. 28), and her works are worthy of praise (29-31).

What does Proverbs 31 say to women today?

How can we keep from being overwhelmed by the "worthy woman?"

Read Philippians 2:3-11

Explain what this verses means to you.

As we direct our lives toward more noble living, we must guard against an elitist attitude in which we think of ourselves more nobly than we think of others (Romans 12:3). Jesus lived a noble life and yet he showed the utmost humility. He was willing to be a sacrifice to give to humanity the salvation we do not deserve. Remembering this will give us more compassion for those whose struggles are greater than ours.

We will have trials. Life will not always be pleasant, for Satan is always tempting us to become disheartened. We need to be aware of his schemes. If we remember that Christ has already won the war over carnality for us, then with prayer we can get through our daily little skirmishes and remain noble and loyal to Christ.

In what area of your life do you need to be more Christlike?

How can we as a group help each other with this need?

How can this group help you individually?

35

Read Proverbs 25:27
Write in your own words.

Although we are told to strive to be noble, we are also warned against seeking honor for ourselves. What a temptation it is to tell the world what good deeds we have done! If you let the world find out for themselves, you will be doubly honored.

Describe a particular person you know who does many good deeds without telling others about it?

DISCUSSION

Define the word, "noble."

How should this word, noble, relate to how we think about God?

List several ways we can keep our thoughts directed toward noble things?

What happens when we "hide our heads in the sand," believing that if we live nobly, we will never suffer?

What repercussions have you had by ignoring some situation with which you should have dealt?

Assignment: This week we will concentrate our thinking on "whatever is noble" and live noble lives. Let's remember "thought transferal" as we try to think on a higher plane and act as if we are "nobility." Be sure to make notes of other's responses and how you feel as you live nobly. We will be eager to hear the reports next week.

Memory verse: Isaiah 32:8

Leader calls on someone to lead closing prayer.

Prayers Answered:

_____
_____
_____
_____
_____
_____
_____
_____
_____

Prayer Requests: _____

_____
_____
_____
_____
_____
_____
_____
_____
_____
_____
_____
_____

Memory Verse:

_____

_____

_____

_____

_____

_____

_____

_____

_____

SESSION 5

❀

THINK ON THINGS RIGHT
PHILIPPIANS 4:8

1. Leader may assign scriptures to be read aloud in class when she calls for them.

2. Begin class with each participant reporting prayers answered and prayer requests (List on page 49).

3. Time of prayer.

4. Give each participant opportunity to tell of her experiences as she practiced being noble.

LEADER PRESENTS LESSON

Our word for today is translated "right, "just," or "good" in the different translations. In modern usage, the word "right" means correct and "just" means fair. When we think of "good," we usually think of "satisfactory in quality."

The Greek work for righteous as used in Philippians 4:8 means "fulfilling all claims which are right and becoming. A right state so that no fault or defect can be charged. (Used of God, it refers to His doings as answering to the rule which He has established for Himself.) Hence, of man it is just, conformity to God's revealed will and also the act of God establishing a man as righteous.

Is there a difference in God's rightness and man's rightness? Explain your answer.

Read Romans 3:10
Rewrite and discuss what this verse means to you.

Yes, God is perfect, so His rightness cannot be improved upon. Man can never be perfectly righteous or even understand God's righteousness.

Read Hosea 14:9
What does Hosea's message mean to you?

The wise walk righteously in the ways of the Lord, and they understand that this is the best way to go. God gives a warning that the rebellious will not have a smooth walk, but will stumble. If you have ever drifted in your faith, you will remember the stumbling that followed. Only by returning to righteousness can we feel we are on a safe course.

Read Psalm 33:4, 5

Rewrite these verses in your own words.

The psalmist assures us that God is faithful in all that he does and that his word is true. How pleased He must be when he sees his children following his example of righteousness and justice. How blessed we are when we feel his unfailing love filling the earth as we extend it to others.

Explain ways we can extend God's righteousness to others?

Read Proverbs 9:9; 20:7
Coordinate these two verses into a one sentence lesson.

A wise man grasps wise instruction and becomes wiser. He is ever adding to his learning. Not only is he prompted to live a right life, but his children are learning to live righteously after him. God instructs the Israelites to teach their children how to live so the chain of learning goes from one generation to the next. If we don't effectively teach those who follow us, God's righteousness will die with us.

Read Hebrews 10:26; Romans 5:5-8; I John 1:7
Combine these verses to make one message about the importance of living right.

God demands that we be right in every aspect of our lives.
Find passages that show how God helps us with this.

He instructs us to live as nearly as we can by the standard Christ set forth when he was here on earth. Can we live a perfect life? No, but He has built in a protection for us when we fail to measure up? What is that protection? The blood of Christ.

Give passages that show how we contact Christ's blood.

Does the blood of Christ take care of willful sins? It took care of David's when he repented, but there were dire consequences for David. That should be a warning to us that willful sinning is not the way to please God. II Samuel 12:13, 14

Read Ephesians 4:24, 32; 5:1, 2; I John 4:12, 19-21
Write a paragraph including the meaning of these verses.

When we come to know God, we put on a new self of righteousness and holiness and we should then be righteous just as God is. We strive to live rightly and love as Christ does. With us it is an ongoing process. We are ever-growing toward righteousness.

How can we keep from getting discouraged when we realize we have not displayed righteousness as Christ did?

We must remember that our lives are a work in progress and rely on God to help us to be more righteous. He is ever patient with us so we need to be patient with ourselves.

DISCUSSION

What does it mean to be just?

Do right and just mean something different in your understanding of the words. Explain your answer.

What is the difference in God's rightness and man's rightness?

Find passages to show that God desires us to be right in every aspect of our lives.

How is there a difference in God's justice (rightness) to us and our justice (rightness) toward each other?

Assignment: The assignment this week is to think on "whatever is right" and be aware of being right in everything we say and do. Keep account of your experiences as you practice right living and write down every day how well you have met the challenge. At the beginning of class next week, you will have opportunity to report any changes this has made in your life.

Memory verse: Revelation 15:3b

Leader calls on someone for closing prayer.

Prayers Answered:

_____

_____

_____

_____

_____

_____

_____

_____

_____

_____

Prayer Requests: _____

_____

_____

_____

_____

_____

_____

_____

_____

_____

_____

_____

Memory Verse:

_____

_____

_____

_____

_____

_____

_____

_____

_____

_____

SESSION 6

❀

THINK ON THINGS PURE
PHILIPPIANS 4:8

1. Leader may assign scriptures to be read aloud in class when she calls for them.

2. Allow time for memory verse to be written in notebooks.

3. Each participant gives report on prayers answered and prayer requests of the class (List on page 61).

4. Time of prayer. Leader may call on one person to give thanks and a second to make the requests of the group.

5. Give each participant opportunity to relate experiences the past week as she practiced right thinking.

LEADER PRESENTS LESSON

It's interesting that of all the words listed in Philippians 4:8, "pure" is the only one that is translated the same in all the common versions. There are three words that are translated "pure" in the New Testament.

How do you define "pure"?

The word used here is defined as:

"Chaste, clean, not contaminated by anything in itself really evil; pure from every defilement."

In Barclay's Daily Study Bible he defines "pure" **as "that which is morally pure. When used ceremonially, it describes that which has been so cleansed that it is fit to be brought into the presence of God and used in the service of God"**

The most common word translated "pure" means free from every foreign admixture, whether good or bad; clean, and free from every stain, odor, color, or any useless thing whatever, free from every false adornment.

When we consider the definition of pure and thinking on things that are pure, it can seem like a great challenge. In our society today, the word has lost its meaning as described in the New Testament. But the people of that age were as far from pure living as the majority of our society , so Paul was giving them as much of a challenge as it is for us.

Read James 3:17; I John 3:2, 3, I Timothy 5:22
Combine these verses to make an abbreviated lesson.

James says that wisdom—true wisdom from above is first of all, pure. And wisdom from above is what Christians are seeking to attain. Worldly wisdom accounts for little in our thoughts and in our actions, but the wisdom from above is pure first, then it has the attributes of peace-loving, considerate, submissive, full of mercy and good fruit, impartial, and sincere.

How does the purity of a Christian's wisdom differ from wisdom of the world?

Paul warns Timothy not to share in the sins of others, but to keep himself pure. His warning is in regard to our relationship with others. We are not to share in their sins, rather we are to lift them to a higher plane and influence them to think pure thoughts, too.

John admonishes us that our hope is in seeing God and knowing him as he is. He instructs that if we have this hope we will purify ourselves as Christ is pure.

We are constantly barraged with sexual impurity. It is important that we take steps to keep the filth out of our homes and away from our children. They are exposed to it at school, on the playground, and on the streets. Home should be the one safe haven where they do not have to contend with filth, the place where they are exposed to purity and encouraged to think pure thoughts.

Discuss ways we can guard our children from impure thoughts.

Read Ephesians 4:29; Colossians 3:8
Combine these verses and rewrite them together.

If we are constantly putting filth into our minds, then unwholesome words are going to come out of our mouths. We must replace the bad with what will build others up. And we are to be aware of what others need, then say and act toward them in a way that will benefit them.

To keep ourselves pure, we must rid ourselves of those things listed in Colossians 3:8. Using filthy language is the result of listening to it until it becomes a part of our speech. It is very easy for our ears to become desensitized.

Have you ever been aware of using a word that in the past you thought was filthy or crude, but over time, you find yourself using it? What influences bring this about?

What can we do to guard against slipping into this practice?

Read II Peter 2:7-10; James 1:21
Rewrite these words, unifying the meaning.

Peter gives Lot as an example of one who was tormented by the un-righteousness (impurity) of those around him. God rescued Lot and He will rescue us, too. If we keep our thoughts on things pleasing to God, then in spite of what goes on around us, we can keep our hearts pure. I often hear someone say it's hard to keep their speech pure when they work with people who are constantly using filthy language. But Lot did and we can, too by asking for God's help.

How can we replace moral filth within our hearts?

We must crave the pure word in order to grow to maturity (I Peter 2:1-3). Daily study will keep our hearts filled with God's goodness.

Read Romans 1:24; I Thessalonians 4:1-7
Rewrite these verses in your words.

The world views sexual purity as a joke. Young girls are often belittled for being virgins. The world is so full of smutty, sordid, shabby ideas that the worldly person cannot even understand the meaning of purity. Minds are so soiled that their impurity spreads to every area of their lives.

How can we help our young girls to see the importance of keeping ourselves pure?

Part of being sanctified (set apart for God's holy purpose) is avoiding sexual immorality or any kind of impurity (Ephesians 5:3). This includes thoughts and actions.

As Paul is instructing the Thessalonians how to live in a manner pleasing to God, he says they should learn to control their own bodies. He says we are called to live pure, holy lives.

Often girls will defend their sexual activities by saying, "We didn't go 'all the way,'" but the Ephesians passage says to avoid even the "hint" of sexual impurity. All of this is improper for God's people. This indeed means we must stay on a higher plane than the world.

Read Colossians 3:1
Write this verse in words you will remember.

In contrast, Christians should set their hearts on things above, clean thoughts and actions that can stand even the scrutiny of God. At any time, we should be able to lay our thoughts before God and not be ashamed of what He sees.

Have you ever been laughed at because you expressed a pure thought without even realizing that the world in general thinks differently about it? On such occasions, we can see that we are set apart for God's holy purpose.

How do you feel if you are made fun of because you express a pure thought?

Remember the definition of the Greek word: "not contaminated by anything in itself really evil; pure from every defilement." Should not our lives be as Barclay said, "so clean that we are fit to be used in the service of God?" Should that not indeed be the purpose of our lives?

DISCUSSION

Name some synonyms of pure. Or give the definition in your own words.

In what way are we to keep our lives pure?

How does the world view purity in contrast with how God teaches it in His word?

Assignment: This week we will strive to be pure in our thoughts and our actions, remembering that we are to be fit to be in the presence of God for indeed we are there all the time. Write down any remarkable things you hear or do relating to purity or impurity in your own life or the lives of others. Next week we will each report on how this exercise has prompted us to act.

Memory verse: I Timothy 1:5

Leader calls on someone to lead the closing prayer.

Prayers Answered:

_____
_____
_____
_____
_____
_____
_____
_____
_____

Prayer Requests: _____

_____
_____
_____
_____
_____
_____
_____
_____
_____
_____
_____
_____

Memory Verse:

_____

_____

_____

_____

_____

_____

_____

_____

_____

_____

SESSION 7

✤

THINK ON THINGS LOVELY
PHILIPPIANS 4:8

1. Leader may assign scriptures to be read aloud in class when she calls for them.

2. Allow time for memory verse to be written in notebook.

3. Each participant reports on prayers answered and prayer requests (List on page 71).

4. Time of prayer.

5. Go around the circle and give each opportunity to relate her experiences as she practiced thinking on pure thoughts all week. How did it change her actions toward others.

LEADER PRESENTS LESSON.

The word "lovely" is used only this one time in the New Testament. The Greek definition is "dear to anyone, pleasing, agreeable." William Barclay says that "winsome is the best translation of all...that which calls forth love..." He says "the Christian is set on the lovely things—kindness, sympathy, forbearance, love—so that the Christian is a winsome person, whom to see is to love."

"Lovely" seems to carry the meaning of calling forth love, attracts to itself, the graciousness that wins and charms.

63

Read I Peter 3:3 , 4

Rewrite how you would say this today.

All of us as women put effort into presenting ourselves as a lovely person. This is an important goal for most of us. It is indeed a compliment if someone says we are lovely.

Beauty is skin deep, but lovely comes from the inside. If it is only outward adornment of pretty clothes, nice skin and shiny hair, or even a sweet smile, it is soon discovered that we are not genuinely lovely. These things may attract others to us for a short time, but they are not lasting traits that help us to make long lasting relationships.

Think of a woman you think of as lovely. Share the attributes that make her lovely.

The word "beautiful" is used three times in the New Testament. In Matthew 23:27 where Jesus tells the Pharisees they are like whitewashed tombs, "beautiful on the outside, but on the inside are full of dead men's bones and everything unclean." This is not how we aspire to be viewed.

The only time "beautiful" is used in the New Testament describing people is in Romans 10:15 about the feet of those who preach the gospel. The literal meaning of the word is "seasonable, as produced or ripened at the fit season...as used of ripe fruit."

Loveliness comes from the inside when we display that "gentle and quiet spirit."

How is "beautiful" generally used in modern language?

Read I Timothy 2:9
How would you express this teaching today?

Our clothing, accessories, and hairstyle are outward expressions of what we are on the inside and whether we are trying to profess godliness in our lives.

It does matter how we present ourselves to others. If first impressions are good, we're on the way to having a positive influence on others. If they are bad, it may take a long time for us to overcome this initial picture we present.

Give an example of someone you have thought of as lovely, only after you have gotten to know her.

Have you ever known someone who you thought was ugly until you got to know them? We moved into a new neighborhood, and I met a neighbor across the street. My first impression was how ugly she was. She was well-kept but her features were not pleasing to the eye. As we became friends, I no longer noticed. I came to love and appreciate her for her inner self. One day as I was thinking about her lovely attributes, my first impression of her came back to my mind. I wondered why I had thought she was so ugly for I now thought of her as a lovely, gentle spirit who was full of good deeds, and she no longer looked ugly in any sense of the word.

How can we keep from judging others by their physical appearance?

Read I Corinthians13:13; John 13:34, 35; John 15:9-12
Rewrite the message from these verses about love.

Because "lovely" comes from the same root word as "love," let's look at its meaning. The Greek noun, "agape," translated "love" in English is never used in common Greek writing, but only in the New Testament. Bullinger says it denotes "love which springs from admiration and veneration...which chooses its object with decision of will and devotes a self-denying and compassionate devotion to it."

God wants us to be lovely because we represent him to those around us. If we present ourselves as gracious and lovely, letting our holiness show through, it will give others a warm and receptive feeling about Christianity.

Read John 21:15-17
Rewrite this as you would ask the question.

We can express our love to others without having that magnetic quality of loveliness, but there is something missing that is very pleasing and attractive if we don't show the warmth and winsomeness that comes when our hearts are full of concern for others as Jesus always was. In the passage above, Jesus is showing Peter that love is more than just lip service. Love is lasting and endures through hard times as well as good times. If our hearts truly love, it is evident through our outer actions.

Read I Corinthians 13:4-7
Rewrite in your words.

The lovely Christian's mind is set on lovely things—kindness, sympathy, forbearance, love. These qualities make her a winsome person. Others enjoy her company and desire to spend time with her. "To know her is to love her."

As with every phase of our lives, loveliness begins in the heart with our thoughts before we can express them to others, and act them out in our interaction with them.

DISCUSSION

What comes to mind when you hear the word, "lovely?"

Why would God want us to think "lovely thoughts?" Why would he want us to be lovely inside?

Can you be a loving person and not be lovely? How?

What attracts you to others before you really know them?

Assignment: This week we will think on things lovely and present ourselves as a lovely person. Remember to practice "thought transferal". If you find yourself thinking things which are not in harmony with God's will, quickly replace it with something that is.

Memory verse: I Peter 3:3,4

Prayers Answered:

_____
_____
_____
_____
_____
_____
_____
_____
_____

Prayer Requests: _____

_____
_____
_____
_____
_____
_____
_____
_____
_____
_____
_____
_____

Memory Verse:

_____

_____

_____

_____

_____

_____

_____

_____

_____

_____

SESSION 8

❋

THINK ON THINGS ADMIRABLE
PHILIPPIANS 4:8

1. Leader may assign scriptures to be read aloud in class when she calls for them.

2. Allow time for memory verse to be written in notebook.

3. Each participant reports on prayers answered and prayer requests (List on page 83).

4. Time of prayer.

5. Go around the circle and give each opportunity to relate her experiences as she practiced thinking on lovely thoughts all week. How did it change her actions toward others.

LEADER PRESENTS LESSON.

The Greek word which is translated as "admirable" in the New International Version is rendered differently in other versions as "good report," "gracious," "honorable" and "good."

Vine's Greek Dictionary defines the word as "uttering words or sounds of good omen, then avoiding ill-omened words, and hence fair-sounding," "of good report," "good report" as "well spoken, well-worded; hence, of good import."

The word translated here as "admirable" is used only one other time in the New Testament in Acts 10:22 describing Cornelius, the centurion. They said, "He is a righteous and God-fearing man, who is respected by all the Jewish people."

Thoughts that are "admirable" are noble, appealing, and fair-sounding. Admirable ideas are worthy of a Christian's thoughts, and we would not be ashamed for God to hear them. They have a high standard of morality.

Read Romans 12:14, 15
Comment on how these verses portray an "admirable" spirit.

When we concentrate on thinking admirable thoughts, we are going to "rejoice with those who rejoice" and never let envy and jealousy creep into our minds. This may be a situation where we can use "thought transferal" to our benefit.

With admirable thoughts we can give a blessing to those who persecute us and say evil against us. We can look at all men as God's creation and know there is good in all, even though we sometimes let the devil inject his way of thinking into our minds. Looking for and expecting the best of others is part of thinking admirable thoughts.

How hard is it for you to think admirable thoughts about someone who seems very different from you? What helps you to do this?

Read Romans 12:3; James 2:1-4
How can these verses help us to have an admirable quality?

God created all of us equal and He has a purpose for all of us. We should avoid trying to elevate ourselves above others. The humble man is following Jesus' example. If we are to be elevated, let others see our good works and offer us a "good seat." We can look very foolish to others if we are always pointing out our good deeds and bragging about our capabilities.

Can you tell of a time when you have seen a humble person elevated? Share how they reacted.

Read Philippians 2:14, 15
Rewrite this to express an admirable personality.

We must fill our minds with innocent thoughts of willingness to serve. What do we have to complain about when we remember all that Jesus did for us? We all know humble servants who "shine like stars in the universe" because of their good attitude about the service they do. We see them admirably creating situations to do things with a true servant's heart.

Read James 3:13-18
Write a sentence expressing what this verse teaches about wisdom.

James says the wise man shows it by his good life. Negative thinking is of the devil. Disorder comes into our lives because of envy and selfish ambition. Those who constantly are negative often end up with physical illnesses, and doctors tell us that being happy, especially developing the habit of laughing, helps us maintain good health.

What are admirable traits you appreciate in another Christian?

Read Ephesians 6:21, 22; Colossians 4:12-17
Rewrite emphasizing the admirable traits Paul is showing.

Paul never misses the opportunity to encourage those who have served him and the Lord in an admirable way. He knows that Tychicus will encourage them. He sets an example to stay in touch with brethren he has worked alongside and to recommend them to others where they are.

He commends Epaphras to the Colossians and says Epaphras prays for their maturity. We pray for those we are concerned about. It's hard to feel ill-will for someone if you keep them in your prayers.

Read Philemon 8-21

Rewrite explaining Paul's plea for admirable Philemon.

Paul expressed a true optimism as he asks Philemon to accept Onesimus back. Optimism is truly an admirable characteristic. How richly we can bless others if we see the good in them and in the situation.

Optimism is an admirable trait we can develop if we make up our minds to look at the bright side of things. Do we look at the glass as half full or half empty? It's better to be a "cockeyed optimist" than a "down in the mouth pessimist." We can work on this as we continue in this course.

Our thoughts can make an enemy or a friend of another person. If we begin to think negative of someone, this will probably continue no matter what they do, unless we make a concentrated effort to think positive of them. If we look for the best, it helps us to maintain a right relationship with others, even with people we do not like at first.

Give an example of qualities in a person you do not admire and share how you try to keep them from becoming a part of your life.

Read James 4:1-6

Express Paul's instructions to make us more admirable.

Looking at Christ, we see Him thinking admirable, honorable thoughts about those whom others were looking down upon. In John 4 when he encountered the Samaritan woman, she expected him to condemn her, but he saw potential in her and gave her hope that she could overcome her sins.

In Matthew 19:14 he used the little children as an example of how we should be. Even though the disciples rebuked them and tried to turn them away, Jesus saw their pure hearts and wanted them around him.

In Luke 23:34 when he was being hung on the cross, he said, "Father forgive them, for they do not know what they are doing."

All of his actions began with thoughts in his heart. Our actions, too, begin with thoughts in our hearts.

DISCUSSION

Name some things that fall into the category of "admirable things" about which we can think.

Make a comparison between the attitudes of an optimist and a pessimist and how they affect our thinking about things that are admirable.

How does our thinking, positive or negative, affect our feelings toward others and our relationship with them?

Looking at the life of Christ, cite examples when we see Him thinking admirable, honorable thoughts and the actions these thoughts precipitate.

Assignment: This week we will practice thinking things that are admirable about others and about situations. Make note of your experiences as you try to turn every negative thought into a positive one. Remember "thought transferal."

Next week we will share with the class how this experience has helped us be more positive in thought and action.

Memory verse: Proverbs 31:30

Leader will call on someone to lead the closing prayer.

Prayers Answered:

_____
_____
_____
_____
_____
_____
_____
_____
_____
_____

Prayer Requests: _____

_____
_____
_____
_____
_____
_____
_____
_____
_____
_____
_____
_____

Memory Verse:

_____

_____

_____

_____

_____

_____

_____

_____

_____

_____

SESSION 9

❀

IF ANYTHING IS EXCELLENT
OR PRAISEWORTHY
PHILIPPIANS 4:8

1. Leader may assign scriptures to be read aloud in class when she calls for them.

2. Allow time for memory verse to be written in notebook.

3. Each participant reports on prayers answered and prayer requests (List on page 95).

4. Time of prayer.

5. Go around the circle and give each person an opportunity to relate her experiences as she practiced thinking on admirable thoughts all week. How it changed her actions toward others.

LEADER PRESENTS LESSON

The word translated "excellent" is defined in the Greek language as "that which gives man his worth, his efficiency, his moral excellence." This is the only time that Paul uses the word in all of his writings.

The word translated "praise" is defined as "praised upon, applause, approbation, commendation." A different word is used in the New Testament when spoken of God, and that word is used only of praise to God

When Paul asks "if anything is excellent or praiseworthy," he is not questioning if there are such things, rather he is exclaiming that there is excellence and praiseworthiness, hence, he is challenging the Philippians to find these things, to fill their thoughts with these highest ideals. Paul links these two concepts together as if he is treating them as one. In our study we, too, will treat them as one, believing that if something is "excellent," it naturally follows that it is also "praiseworthy."

When we think of things that are excellent, God's creation comes to mind. He created everything in a perfect setting. And even though man has abused it through the centuries, it is still in a very functional, beautiful, excellent state.

Other things in our lives that are excellent include the goodness of others, great feats that mankind has accomplished, the kindnesses extended by God's children. Many also develop personalities that are unusually praiseworthy in spite of obstacles that Satan throws in their way.

Read Psalm 19:7-11
Rewrite in capsule form.

Some of us may want to use this scripture as our strength this week as we try to practice thinking excellent thoughts. The psalmist tells us to look to the Lord for our soul's revival, for statutes of trustworthiness. These things will bring joy to our hearts and help us to have a new outlook on life. If we follow the Lord's rules, we will have great reward.

Share with the class several ways to bring praiseworthy thoughts into our minds.

Many of us wonder why we have the troubles we have in everyday life, never looking back to see what we have done in the past to create our present environment. Although we don't want to dwell on past mistakes, it's good to evaluate them to keep from making the same mistakes again.

The wonderful thing is that God will help us to overcome if we trust Him, but when we try to do it ourselves, we are sure to fail. A regular study of God's word will helps us to keep in tune with Him and stay focused on positive thoughts and actions.

It is a human tendency to blame ourselves rather than just repent and put our mistakes in the past. Name ways we can better accept the grace of God's forgiveness?

Read Psalm 119:164-168
Rewrite to make applicable for your life today.

Great peace is ours when we think of the excellence of God's law.
How can we love it unless we are familiar with it and keep it ever present in our minds. There is great value in "waiting on the Lord." Is
it hard for you to just sit and think? Most of us feel that is a waste of
time. In reality there is great value in quietness when we can absorb
something we have read in God's word. He comes to us in these times
and implants thoughts in our minds. He helps us to think through our
problems and arrive at sound solutions. It takes training to be quiet
and listen to God.

List things you do to help you take time to think what God's word is
saying to you?

Read Philippians 1:3-8
List and discuss how this text helps you to think excellent and praiseworthy thoughts.

Paul praised the Philippians for their good work and their carrying the tasks through to completion. Our praise should always be sincere and appropriate. It gives a real boost to all of us to be praised for something we know we have done well. But false or insincere praise only makes the recipient uncomfortable and the giver seem like a phony. A person who is generous with sincere and deserved praise is respected and loved. It's very easy to praise such a one.

What helps you to find ways to praise an individual who is not so desirable?

Romans 13:7; Romans 16:1-4
List and discuss Paul's praise of the individuals named here.

Paul tells us to give honor to whom honor is due, and he gives example by praising many throughout his writings. He was free with his praise to brethren he had known in other places. He praised Phoebe saying she had been a great help to many people. As he sends greetings to the church in Rome, he commends many: Priscilla and Aquilla for their labor with him and for risking their lives for him, Mary (Romans 16:6) for her hard work, and many others in the verses that follow.

Do you find it hard to praise people who have out shone you in some endeavor? Yes_____ No_____
How do you create right thinking toward them?

Read I Peter 2:17
Rewrite and discuss in your words.

Peter emphasizes proper respect and love for the brotherhood. It is appropriate to give praise and honor to those who deserve it. It makes the world a happier place to live. William Barclay said: "A Christian will live in such a way that he will neither conceitedly desire nor foolishly despise the praise of men whose praise is a thing to be desired."

How does it make you feel when you receive worthy praise?

Read II Timothy 1:16-18
Rewrite and discuss Paul's praise to Onesiphorus.

Paul praises the household of Onesiphorus for refreshing him in many ways. It is good to let others know when someone has rendered service. It is appropriate to praise people for what they have done, for their accomplishments, their sweet dispositions.

Worthy praise is appreciated. It helps us to develop strong personalities and makes us try even harder. Praise should be given for accomplishments, a sweet disposition or the way a situation is handled rather than for physical appearance, intellect or characteristics which we are not responsible for developing. God should get the praise for those things.

How can we develop the ability to give praise to whom it is due?

DISCUSSION

What comes to your mind when you think of excellent thoughts?

List ways we can keep our minds centered on excellent, virtuous thoughts when we are surrounded by those whose minds are centered on the vile, immoral things of this world?

If we praise men, for what should we praise them?

And for what should we avoid praising men?

Assignment: This week we will be thinking on things that are excellent and praiseworthy. Make notes of how your thoughts on these things changed your actions and your reactions toward others.

Come to class next week prepared to share your experiences with the class.

Memory verse: Romans 13:7

Leader will call on someone to lead the closing prayer.

Prayers Answered:

_____
_____
_____
_____
_____
_____
_____
_____
_____

Prayer Requests: _____

_____
_____
_____
_____
_____
_____
_____
_____
_____
_____
_____

Memory Verse:

_____

_____

_____

_____

_____

_____

_____

_____

_____

SESSION 10

❀

PUT YOUR THOUGHTS INTO PRACTICE
PHILIPPIANS 4:9

1. Leader may assign scriptures to be read aloud in class when she calls for them.

2. Allow time for memory verse to be written in notebook.

3. Each participant reports on prayers answered and prayer requests (List on page 107).

4. Time of prayer.

5. Go around the circle and give each person opportunity to relate her experiences as she practiced thinking on excellent and praiseworthy thoughts all week. How did it change her actions toward others.

LEADER PRESENTS LESSON

Paul has finished with his list of things we are to think about and now he tells us to put into practice what we have learned from studying these attributes. Let's take time here to reflect on what we have learned. (Leader goes around the circle, giving each one opportunity to tell what she has learned from the study thus far.)

Read Philippians 4:9
Rewrite in your words and discuss.

Paul doesn't stop when he finishes his list of what we are to think. Next he instructs the Philippians that they should put these things into practice. All the knowledge in the world will do us no good unless we DO what we have learned. This is what we have been attempting as we have taken one element each week and put it into practice. Now it's time for us to bring it all together and see how to incorporate all of these attributes into our life as we relate to others day by day.

Read Colossians 3:17
Rewrite and discuss.

This verse shows us that our words and our deeds must synchronize in order for us to live a godly life. It's important that we speak rightly but we must also act out with our deeds what our words convey. We have all known people who are full of flattering words, but their life does not reflect what their words say. This is a form of hypocrisy. Those who live this way are not effective servants of God once they are found out. It is essential that our words and deeds are in harmony.

What changes do you need to make in order to "act in the manner you speak?"

Read Galatians 6:2-5; Romans 12:16

List and discuss how to put our good thoughts into action.

At first glance it might seem there is a contradiction in Galatians 2, verses 2 and 5. First, Paul says we should carry each other's burdens, then he says we should carry our own load. Part of our Christian duty is to lighten the load of those who have fallen. At times we all have a load too heavy to bear alone. This is the time we should step up and help our brothers, but we should not become conceited thinking we are more spiritual than the one who needs help. It is dangerous to compare ourselves to others. Remember Christ is the one we are to pattern our lives after. In so doing, we will be willing to lend a helping hand whenever it is needed.

Paul follows this instruction by telling us we should each carry our own load. We should not ask for help until we need it. We can become dependent on others when we should be more self-sufficient.

So we make every effort to carry our own load, but when we see another who is stumbling because his load is too heavy, then we should willingly help him carry his load. We also need to be humble enough to accept help when we need it.

Is it easier for you to accept help when you really need it or give help to someone elsc who really needs it? Give the reason for your answer.

Read Romans 12:9-13; Ephesians 4:32

Discuss putting these verses into practice.

These scriptures include both thinking and doing what is right. First, we must have love in our hearts for others. We must love the good and hate the evil we encounter each day. We must think good thoughts and then carry them out by honoring others above ourselves. We must have zeal to serve the Lord with a real spiritual fervor.

Thinking good thoughts is incomplete in our service unless we put these thoughts into practice by showing a joyful spirit with hope, extending patience to others (especially when they are afflicted), and praying faithfully.

We must not only have compassionate thoughts toward those who are in need, but we must share with them. Hospitality is such a vital part of Christianity and it is so much neglected today. Because we have become such an affluent society, we are all too into ourselves, thinking we don't need others. But there are many who do need us. Perhaps today there is a bigger need for emotional support and security than there is for financial help. These needs may not be as obvious, but encouragement may be more needed than food to help someone to have a balanced, fulfilling life.

As we learn to control our thoughts, then we will have more compassion for others and be willing to forgive as God forgives, which is vital if we are to live as we should.

100

How do you view the "down and outer?"

How can we be more understanding of those who truly need help?

Read Colossians 3:13

Discuss and record the importance of this teaching today.

We must think good thoughts about others and learn to be tolerant of differences. Conflict comes when our thoughts get out of control and we begin to think the worst of others. That's when "thought trans-feral" works at its best.

Read Hebrews 3:13; Hebrews 10:24, 25
Rewrite and discuss these verses.

Encouraging others will not only help them, but will also aid us in seeing the good in others and acting toward them as God wants. Today is
the time we should practice reassuring others of their value in God's
sight. God has a plan for each of us and we can help others reach their
goals with reassuring words.

Our thoughts toward others should be how we can spur them on to do
even greater things for the Lord than before. We can encourage others
by setting the example of being regular in worship. This is where we
get fed spiritually and fortify our strength for the tough times ahead.
When we meet together it builds us up to face the fiery darts of the
enemy when we are not among Christians.

How important is it to you to be regular in worship? Discuss how you
miss it when you are not able to be there?

DISCUSSION

What happens when we do not put the things we learn into action?

Discuss the correlation between our thoughts and our actions.

Why is it hard for some people to accept help? How can we overcome
this?

What is the two-fold blessing in encouraging others?

Why does God want us to meet together for worship rather than worshiping alone?

Assignment: This week we will be putting into action the thoughts we have been developing in the previous weeks. Let's take every opportunity to act out the good thoughts we have learned to think, to treat others in the way Jesus did.

Come to class next week prepared to share your experiences after you have spent a week trying to do good deeds.

Memory verse: I Thessalonians 3:11, 12

Leader will call on someone to lead the closing prayer.

Prayers Answered:

_____
_____
_____
_____
_____
_____
_____
_____
_____
_____

Prayer Requests: _____

_____
_____
_____
_____
_____
_____
_____
_____
_____
_____
_____

Memory Verse:

_____

_____

_____

_____

_____

_____

_____

_____

_____

SESSION 11

❁

BE CONTENT
PHILIPPIANS 4:11-12

1. Leader may assign scriptures to be read aloud in class when she calls for them.

2. Allow time for memory verse to be written in notebook.

3. Each participant reports on prayers answered and prayer requests (List on page 119).

4. Time of prayer.

5. Go around the circle and give each opportunity to relate her experiences as she practiced trying to put good thoughts we have learned into practice all week. How did she act differently toward others.

LEADER PRESENTS LESSON

Read Philippians 4:10-12
Write and discuss the lesson Paul is teaching the Philippians.

Paul begins this lesson to the Philippians (and us) by reminding us to "Rejoice!" (Philippians 4: 4). Through prayer we can overcome our anxieties by making our requests known to God for everything that concerns us. (verse 6). Then he begins a practical progression of making these things a part of our lives:

[Step 1] Think positive, upbuilding thoughts (verse 8).

[Step 2] Put these wholesome thoughts into practice (verse 9).

[Step 3] Learn to be content (verse 11).

Paul is an example of being content in all circumstances. If Paul can do it, with all he endured in his lifetime, can't we also learn this? The purpose of this whole series of lessons is to put into practice what Paul tells us to do in order that we may be happy serving God and content as Paul was, "whatever the circumstances."

Tell the class of the time in your life you remember being the most content. What were the circumstances that made you content?

Read Psalm 20:7,8

Rewrite and discuss an appropriate comparison for us today.

Do you know anyone who trusts in their chariots and horses today? Probably not, but is this verse not applicable to many you know who trust in their houses, cars, savings, jobs, and other material things? Our society is geared to accumulate "things" which we have been taught by the world will give us security, make our lives easier and more pleasant. But too many times we see everything disappear in an instant. Many times the hurricanes and wildfires wipe out hundreds of acres and many homes. We can lose our savings in a bad investment or a "sour deal." Putting our trust in "things" is false security. Our only security is investing in a good life that will give us that eternal home with God. But right living will not only reward us in the here-after, but it will help make us more contented here.

Discuss struggles you may have in trusting God instead of material things for your security.

Read Proverbs 3:5,6
Rewrite and discuss how you can make these verses your own.

Paul had learned to trust God in all things and we must too, if we want to be content all the time. These verses from Proverbs show that man's wisdom is a fleeting thing unless it is built on God's word. We cannot fully grasp God's ever-present care for us unless we step out on faith and trust Him. Each time we trust Him to see us through something we cannot accomplish without Him, our faith grows and it makes it easier to take the next step.

Relate a time when your life was in turmoil, but you felt at peace because you were relying on God's word.

Read I Timothy 6-10
Rewrite and discuss the teaching here.

True contentment comes only through godly living. We may feel contented for a while with worldly goods, but soon we become restless and want more. We always need just a little more than what we have right now to keep us happy. People in humble circumstances are as likely to be happy as those who have great riches. It is hard for us to grasp this concept when we are young and getting started, but the longer we live, the more we see that as long as we have food, clothing and shelter, we really have all we need.

The truth is that how much we have has little to do with how happy we are. The way we value our earthly belongings has much to do with it. If we see what God has given us as tools to use in our service to Him, then we are content. If we see what we own as security for our life here, then we will always be restless and wanting more. The person who is busy serving God has little time to worry about accumulating wealth. God often blesses us with much more than we can think to ask for when we let go and let Him work in our lives.

Many times our riches lead us into temptation that we know nothing of before we accumulate a lot of this world's goods. With wealth comes the need to protect it. Those who have little of what others desire have little need for security systems, excessive insurance, and enormous safety deposit boxes.

None of these thing are wrong in themselves, but they can become a stumbling block if we put our trust in them. Money is not the root of all kinds of evil. Money is a neutral. It's our attitude toward it, the love of it, that causes evil in our lives.

Those with wealth often become more interested in gaining more and "wander from the faith piercing themselves with many griefs."

Share with the class your greatest temptation to trust in riches.

Read Hebrews 13:5-7
Rewrite and discuss how the teaching affects your thinking and actions.

The writer of Hebrews warns that we must keep our lives free from the love of money. He assures us that God will never leave us. We should have confidence that He will see us through and this should take away our fear of what man can do to us. To put full trust in God is the most liberating lesson we will ever learn. It matters not what man does to us when we know the great Protector is there to help us.

Share a time when you have trusted in God and seen His workings in your life.

We, too, can find the secret of being content if we put our trust in God and work under His leadership and instruction.

DISCUSSION

Give each one opportunity to write, then share with the group a time when they have found it hard to trust God, but in so doing, their faith has grown.

Write and share a time when trusting in possessions has disappointed you and let you down.

Describe below someone you know who has demonstrated a devoted trust in God. Share with the group.

How can we overcome our desire to accumulate more of this world's goods?

What is your greatest hindrance in "being content in all circumstances"?

Assignment: This week we will make every effort to be content with whatever comes our way. Remember "thought transferal" if you begin to feel discontented. Keep notes of your struggles and how you have overcome them to remain contented. Next week we will share with the class the progress we have made and what has helped us to be more contented.

Memory Verse: Psalm 9:10

Leader will call on someone to lead closing prayer.

Prayers Answered:

_____
_____
_____
_____
_____
_____
_____
_____
_____
_____

Prayer Requests: _____

_____
_____
_____
_____
_____
_____
_____
_____
_____
_____
_____
_____
_____
_____

Memory Verse:

_____
_____
_____
_____
_____
_____
_____
_____
_____
_____

SESSION 12

❊

I CAN DO EVERYTHING THROUGH HIM
PHILIPPIANS 4:13

1. Leader may assign scriptures to be read aloud in class when she calls for them.

2. Allow time for memory verse to be written in notebook.

3. Each participant reports on prayers answered and prayer requests (List on page 127).

4. Time of prayer.

5. Go around the circle and give each opportunity to relate her experiences as she practiced being content all week. How did this change her attitude about her life?

6. Leader will open discussion with explanation that everyone will take part in presenting the lesson today.

DISCUSSION

Read Philippians 4:13

Write and discuss what this verses means to you.

It means anything I decide to do spiritually God will give me the strength to do it.

As we begin, let's remember that God is the One who will provide strength for everything that is in His plan for us to do. When we are living for Him, we pray for His guidance—then He shows us what we should do, and He provides the strength. The Bible is full of scripture which assures us of this.

Today we will let God's word speak directly to us. As we take turns reading from His word, we will be reminded again from whence our strength comes. Listed below are a number of passages, from both the Old and New Testament, about God's strength. Most of these are straightforward and need little explanation, so after you read, please make a short comment. (Leader will go around the circle calling on each one to read.)

Old Testament:
Deuteronomy 33:25	Psalm 29:11
II Samuel 22:1-3	Psalm 46:1
II Samuel 22:33	Psalm 105:4
Psalm 18:1, 2	Isaiah 12:2
Psalm 18:30-32	Isaiah 40:28-31
Psalm 28:7	Isaiah 41:10

New Testament:
Luke 22:43	I Thessalonians 3:11-13
I Corinthians 1:25	I Peter 4:11
Ephesians 3:16-19	II Timothy 4:17
I Thessalonians 2: 16, 17	

Read Ephesians 6:10
Discuss how you plan to use this in the future.

Always keep in mind God is in Control if we will let him

122

The Bible is clear on the fact that God is the power behind us and it is only in Him that we find the strength to live for Him. Is His strength of muscles and brawn only? No, in Him we find the mental, emotional, and spiritual strength to function effectively for Him. Being strong in the Lord is even possible for the physically weak.

Is there any correlation between physical strength and spiritual strength? How does one complement the other? *you can be challenged to handle something + need your physical strength to see you through the physical.*

Read II Timothy 2:1

Comment on this advice Paul give Timothy. *— Was young considered a man at 20 —*

Our strength is a portion of the unmerited favor (grace) meted out to us by God. When we think we can do things without his help, we are deceiving ourselves. All of us have probably been guilty of this at times. All good things come from God according to James 1:17. Every day we should give thanks to Him for all the good things in our lives.

What helps you to be aware of God's grace in your everyday life?

Read I Peter 5:10

Rewrite and discuss what this verse means to you.

Even if we suffer — we will get our strength + support from god

God is the One who makes us strong. He gives us the strength to do what He has for us to do. If we direct our strength toward serving Him, then we will always have enough to get the job done. Perhaps we won't have enough to please ourselves, but perhaps we expect more of ourselves than God expects of us. It might be time to re-evaluate our activities, do less, do it better, and feel we have accomplished what He wants of us realizing He is pleased with our efforts.

Share with the group a time that you have felt God's strength in a challenge in your life.

Lost of everything

Assignment: Throughout this week we will take time to realize that our strength comes from God. We will remember that He gives us the strength to do what He wants us to do, realizing that if we are busy for Him and looking for opportunities to serve, He will provide both the opportunities and the strength to complete the tasks.

Next week we will share with the class what our meditation on this lesson has helped us to realize about our life and changes we think we need to make.

Memory Verse: Psalm 46:10

Leader will call on someone to lead closing prayer.

Prayers Answered:

_____
_____
_____
_____
_____
_____
_____
_____
_____

Prayer Requests: _____

_____
_____
_____
_____
_____
_____
_____
_____
_____
_____
_____

Memory Verse:

_____

_____

_____

_____

_____

_____

_____

_____

_____

_____

SESSION 13

❀

GOD WILL MEET ALL YOUR NEEDS
PHILIPPIANS 4:19

1. Leader may assign scriptures to be read aloud when she calls for them.

2. Allow time for memory verse to be written in notebook.

3. Each participant reports on prayers answered and prayer requests (List on page 137).

4. Time of prayer.

5. Go around the circle and give each opportunity to relate her experiences as she remembered all week that she can do everything through Him. Did this help fortify you to launch out and accept new challenges?

LEADER WILL PRESENT LESSON

Read Philippians 4:14-19
Condense and comment on what Paul is saying.

In our lesson last week, Paul makes the bold statement that he can do everything through God who gives him strength. Now he gives his appreciation to the Philippians for helping him do the work that God has set before him. Paul always gives God the credit for his success. God works through many people in many ways to help us to do all things He wants us to do.

God also uses many other people and things to meet all our needs. Often Christian people are heard to say, "I was very lucky." Luck is not the source of good fortune in a Christian's life, for we know that all good gifts come from God (James 1:17). We should change our comment to, "God blessed me richly."

Paul commends the Philippians for meeting his needs and says they are the only ones who did so.

What part did God play in Paul's needs being met?

God provided Paul with what he needed through the Philippians. Paul explains that their gifts will be credited to their accounts. Jesus said: "It is more blessed to give than to receive" (Acts 20:35). This concept is easy to understand when we practice it. The more often we give sacrificially, the more God blesses us in return. You cannot out give God.

With Paul, we should consider each gift an "acceptable sacrifice, pleasing to God."

In claiming the promise that God will meet all our needs, we should examine our list of needs. As we have more, we keep dragging things from our "want list" to our "need list." How different our "need list" is to those who lived in the past. In reality our "need list" is really only food, clothing, and shelter. How richly God has blessed us in that we "need" so much more just to function in today's world. Do we thank Him often enough for all the rich material blessings He has given us today?

DISCUSSION

Discuss the things that you feel are necessities now that were luxuries to your parents when they were your age. How can we become more aware of becoming more content with what we have?

Read Luke 12:48

Rewrite and discuss the meaning.

With each blessing comes new responsibility to serve in a better way. Because God has blessed us so richly, He will expect more from us than from others who do not have as much. We will be rewarded for meeting His expectations. Using our time and talent to serve will bring us great satisfaction.

List and tell the group ways you can improve your service to God because of the way He has blessed you.

Read II Corinthians 9:8

Rewrite and discuss how we can put this verse into action.

When we take a step in faith to do God's will, we soon learn that He WILL meet all our needs. Missionaries who are willing to launch out, not knowing where their support will come from, find that God always provides. Often His help comes from where it is least expected. Stories abound of families on the mission field who lose their support and how, just at the right time, they will receive an unexpected check to carry them through.

God knows what we need and when we need it and often supplies right at the last minute. He will never ask anything of us that He does not supply what we need to complete the task. Whether it be physical strength, mental know-how, or financial means, He promises He will see us through. And when we undertake a task and fail, then prayerfully turn it over to God, He always gives us a better solution than we can think of on our own.

Tell of a time when you have wrestled with a problem, finally giving it to God in prayer, and the results in your life.

Read Psalm 23

Rewrite and discuss making this appropriate for us today.

There is no passage that gives us greater assurance that God will always meet our needs than this psalm. With this great Shepherd we will have no wants. David paints a picture of peace and serenity as we walk with God. I have a friend who has a "prayer garden" in the corner of her yard. This is where she sits daily to read and meditate on His word and to pray to Him. David says God will guide us righteously and that His love and goodness will be with us as we dwell with Him. He is always there to give us peace and help us find a solution to our problems And though shadows may come from time to time, we have nothing to fear.

Tell of your favorite place to be quiet and listen to God.

Assignment: This week we will make a list of times when God has supplied our needs in a particular way that we did not expect and remember them to share with the class when we meet again soon. We will share with one another how these incidences have strengthened our faith.

Next week we will share with the class what our meditation on this lesson has helped us to realize about our life and changes we think we need to make.

Memory Verse: Philippians 4:19

Leader will call on someone to lead closing prayer.

Prayers Answered:

Prayer Requests:

REFLECTIONS & ANTICIPATION

To further enhance this course, the group should share a buffet together soon after the last meeting and giving each participant opportunity to summarize what she has gained from participation in the course and how it has affected her life.

The leader will arrange for a time and a place to meet for the meal. After the previous twelve sessions, each participant should feel comfortable sharing with the entire group what the course has meant in her life. Each one should come prepared to make a short talk as her final part in the course. It enriches the rewards of the course if each participant stands to address the group.

In order for each one to take away the most lasting gain from the course, the group should spend time reflecting on the study, its lasting meaning, and how they plan to continue practicing what they have learned.

End the evening with prayer requests and a chain prayer including the whole group.